SEVEN

ANTONIO J. HOPSON

ANAPHORA LITERARY PRESS

ATLANTA, GEORGIA

ANAPHORA LITERARY PRESS
1803 Treehills Parkway
Stone Mountain, GA 30088
http://anaphoraliterary.com

Book design by Anna Faktorovich, Ph.D.

Edited by: Katie Doemland

Cover Image: "7 of Hearts" by Tony Meeuwissen

Published in 2015 by Anaphora Literary Press

Seven
Antonio J. Hopson—1st edition.

Print ISBN-13: 978-1-68114-095-7
ISBN-10: 1-681140-95-0
EBook ISBN-13: 978-1-68114-096-4
ISBN-10: 1-681140-96-9

Library of Congress Control Number: 2015941134

SEVEN

ANTONIO J. HOPSON

To the boys...

It is said that throughout all of human history, there are only seven stories to tell: overcoming the monster, rags to riches, voyage and return, the quest, comedy, tragedy, and rebirth…

I am a lover. A gentleman. A pirate. A father of two boys and the ex-husband of a suicidal addict who survived breast cancer. Life is a journey, and part of the time we are on fire, or laughing, making love, drinking, watching crows fuck. I've embedded all seven of my stories into a single book of poetry. Here are my selections.

Men Like Me

(To be read loudly! With bravado! With punch! (And I recommend first eating a spoonful of hot Chinese mustard.))

I would fight through
the hounds of hell
and wounds of flesh
to be blessed by the simplicity of your smile.
So many warriors
of love
and less
have died
and will die
not knowing the touch of this simple thing.
They say it is symmetry,
and I laugh out loud at them,
the fools who do not know the wicked and wacky and
wonderful things a woman can hide behind such a fulgent
gate. They do not know that
there is love there too.
To be captured by these men!
Men like me.
Men like me. Who storm the gate, mad with love. Mad with
it.
Cannon fodder and shrapnel
in their faces
piercing their heart-shrouded
neuro-transmissions of lust and frosting and love and
wonder and pain and suffering
and pleasure
and the cry of ghosts
and the smell of grass
and salted sea water kisses that taste of tears falling from the
moon in a dream that can never be dreamt without the light.

The spark.
That smile.
The one that started the whole damn thing in the first place.
I am not ashamed to be in this league of gentlemen and
pirates, of dorks and jackasses.
We know
that you know just as well
that we are fools for the pleasure of your smile.

I Steal

I steal
glances of you
through my lightning box.
The one with the power to hold open the hard fixtures of
time and space
of which I am traveler.
I seek the thread that connects us
through the maw of darkness where awaits a burnished,
resplendent blush…
I steal glances of you
and I smile
like a jeweler setting stones
in silver.
From time to time, I walk my eyes through the box and let
them sting and water until I can
feel the connection pulsing
like a living, distant neutron star, never cold
never alone
in a sky of galaxies
holding their jewels like children in a billion tender cradles
rocked gently
with a single fingertip.
I steal glances and I will steal more.
When the box is closed
I will see you in candlelight
or huddled next to a small fire
or under this starry night.

I Mourn You

I mourn your carefree kisses
your careful touch.
Your urgent eyes
ever and ever happy.
I mourn your sublime curves,
and being lost in them without a care...living from one tiny
fire to the next.
I mourn your bed, and the warmth I found there
the smell of your body
unbathed
without sin.
It lingers on me like a musk
A secret
left abaft, perfumed in
woe and joy and nonsense.
I mourn the disgrace and pleasure of your punishments...
blazes that settled into solicitude and tenderness.
I mourn the moment when I could not see your subtle
redress
...a scent, left lingering in our holy space.

A Kiss

A smile
can travel
a thousand miles
but a touch is now
revealing its
Epicurean delights.
From closed eyelids
down the cheek
to the dimple and chin
a trail…
where kisses belong.

"For You"

Though
distant...
I die
in your
gaze tonight...
Through the blaze
and smoke
of the fire
I've built,
besieged
by crystal ice.
The place where our hearts first met
and now are
consumed.
Buried
alive,
together
in
snow.

Hope

I wish to
cry myself to sleep
and
awaken
on the sea that I have wept.

That Burning Bush I Saw

In an orange-spangled fire
burning there,
between two highways
two seasons
joining our dimension to the next:
a sovereign, lonely thing.
Touched by its own failing flesh
crying a river too.
Had I seen it
or it me?
And, if you are there
or were...
Why haven't you come to visit me again?

Silver

This is my favorite picture of you
your gold-spun hair fashioned into a bun
your pink lips smiling
me into the future…
I'm waiting for you to find me lost in a supine forest
crowded with lush ferns
dripping with dew drops
waiting to fall
to the soft
thirsty earth.
And when you find me
you are holding something marvelous in your hand
a trinket with a key
to your gentle heart.
I know you are waiting for a love like me
because I am waiting for you
to fall into the same trap of time and space
as it meanders over the mountains
wiggling in stars
and a black, black night.
Like your hazel eyes,
set in silver
against
the cream of your skin.

Thoughts on Whiskey and Love

Knock hard
or ring the bell twice.
Knock hard
slink into my home.
You are invited in.
Undress.
Chin…chin.

A Poet is a Fool

Left on the mountain
Moses on the mound
a poet is a fool
a fool with a sliver crown
a poet is a saved child
a liar
and a clown
afraid to let the good days go
and die
without a sound…

Invited Guest

You are right.
keeping your hands off things that do not belong to you
is a virtue.
And the moon is far away
by design.
You are not to touch it
unless invited.
You are invited.
Your ancestors whisper
because they are telling you a secret.
Not a lie.
You need a hand.
Not forgery.
The world is wanton.
Its images a wake
left in a star-crossed trail.
But you have a lens
to see,
a heart
to feel.
And I know you are an animal.
I can smell you.
Or wish to.
Your neck...
Your chin...
Your bosom...
My honey is there.
And inside of me,
where my mind dreams up these foolish possibilities.
They do not come from an animal, do they?
Not a bear in the woods, nor a lioness in a cage, can dream
of things and make them real...
like drunkards dancing in moonlight for no good reason...

to touch and see and feel the dream entering our bodies
together
through gooseflesh
and tiny hairs that stand up on the skin without a clue.
Still they stand.
For us.
To send us to the moon...
invited guests.

A Murder of Crows

A hopeful cawing began as the creatures in the grove
picked and preened through phantom pictures of meals.
Somewhere in their cognizance, they visualized dropped
sticky sweets left on the beach, or the butt-ends of crumbly
hot dog buns, purple gum, chicken bones with gristle. They
dreamed, or perceived to dream, of fattened squirrels and
cats left dead in the city's streets: spines, a limb or two—
something that would sustain them, body and soul. In their
mind's eyes they stood over the carcasses and culled flesh
from the bones and flew into the clouds with dangling
entrails from their beaks.
In their black eyes, one could see morning's sun rising into
sweet rapture.

Some of the creatures were not interested in food at all. Some
dreamed of sex—sex in the trees, sex on a telephone wire, in
an old dusty attic, on a chimney. While the sun continued
to rise, these birds preened themselves in foppish detail and
picked obsessively at feathers in the pits of their wings.

Then there were those who dreamed of war—war with big
birds, war with little birds, war with medium birds, war with
a fence post. They schemed: a fierce talon in the eye followed
by deadly pecking? Or a beak in the eye, followed by a
deadly clawing? Who their foe would matter very little, so
long as blood be spilt this day!

As the sky ignited, rays of light began to crest the city's
skyscrapers, sending golden warmth into the moss-covered
thicket. Shadows from the new light drifted through knotted
limbs and made branches crawl like snakes. In a moment, it
would be time to fly.

The birds readied themselves.

They bounced on their perches, exercising cramped muscles. Some called out crass serenades, exciting themselves, and others dropped onto rooftops and began pulling at shingles small and loose enough to molest.

The denizens in their houses heard the cawing, the clatter, the clawing and the torn, fallen *clang!* of shingles sliding into tin gutters. Dreary-eyed, they turned off their electric alarm clocks, rolled out of bed, dressed, and in silence, joined the murder.

Again

The sight of your hungry mouth,
my breath is stolen
ripe as fruit,
hungry for moisture.
I am starved to make them part.
I am starved to make them moist,
again.
If only to feel the hot, damp wind of the tropics soothing my
skin,
for there is where I arose,
and long to be,
with you,
and soon I will return.
I awaken
gazing into our stars:
There is my king, Jupiter.
There is your queen, Venus.
I look back to you
tender as our stars.
Forever cold, they do not fall for us.
But closer…
closer still.
The twinkle becomes consuming
and I am lost in your warmth
again.

Go Ahead and Fall

Into the mystery
where so quietly
we think
in a metal leeway
without a ridge
or cover
here…
our hearts are synchronized…
their clocks timed
to the sound of a single
falling
penny
into a vessel
of riveted walls,
where we have
things to cherish
and more metal than hope,
it falls.
And we are falling too.
Waiting for it to land
and sing
then dance
and settle
then rest
and sleep there…carelessly waiting
to hear the sound of again.
When it does
we will listen together.
and sing beyond these walls
I heard it too.

Bleach

I now know the sting of your poison.
The acid and sour scold and seeping wounds you leave
unsatisfied by peace
yet attracted to love.
There have been a thousand lies
gifted to me as truth,
The lure of your undying love a trap
which closes like a gentle black drape until all the light is
gone
and I am left with your puzzles
your many attempts to quiet me while I listen to your
blustering, confused hatred
interrupted by the attention of all those men you have
bedded
or who wish to bed you
waiting for your boredom
with me this time.
When I am gone
and this will be soon
you will have them
(you already do)
and they will continue to tell you the things a tiger likes to
hear
and I will be gone.
My fire
the one I always lit for you,
is now buried in the ash of what was once love.
And, though large pieces of me are missing,
I never failed respecting you enough to tell
My truth.
The truth your lust cannot swallow.
Did not swallow.
I have suffered the look of men confused by my willingness

to let you be,
let you curse and dance and then turn on me when it is time
to leave the feast.
And now I know.
After you read this,
I will never allow you to stomp on my little fire again.
For now I know you are envious of it.
You threw shoes at it, you screamed at it, howled and
laughed at it.
Blind as a stone and just as destructive.
You have channeled your anger on me, focused it,
Tornados have no need to say I'm sorry.
I would say I'm sorry too, but I already know what you're
going to say.
This hell, it's like fighting in the mirror with tar-drenched
torches at night.
So here is my torch.
I give it to you to cherish.

Speechless

I am low on words
But the sting is here.
The bite.
I am in love with you.
It cannot change.
No matter how repeated the words
the goodness of being lost in your magic
your spell remains.
The stars are cold
…watching us.
The wind blows nothing
nothing at all.
But still there is the sting.
less these words.
Because I can only understand it when I am once again
entombed,
lost in your smoky gaze
my senses are full
lustful for the smooth, silken wonderment of your skin
and the thrill of your touch.
I am less of words,
but still traveling in time.
Falling
together
with you...

When Trumpets Lie

The trumpet was designed to fail.
All its songs are sad.
The thing has started many wars
and is there to close them, too.
When has a trumpet ever brought you good news?
Jazz is not good news.
It was built on the back of the blues
And blues is sadness
jazzed up for whites to earn a paycheck.
stories of rape and labor made palatable by medicating
spoonfuls of misery,
blown through a stolen instrument.
The same instrument used to announce the privilege of the
hunt.
In fact, the only happy trumpet I ever heard was played by a
cool-ass jazz teacher struggling to keep it in its place.
When a trumpet is heralding life, it is reborn as death.
Play the same song slower
and you will see.
There is nothing noble about this instrument.
The dirtier it sounds, the better it is.
Like a cursing princess in torn-up boots.
How I despise thee trumpet
except when you play "Tequila"
a drinking song about a dirty town filled with drugs and
death and street-food venders who'd sell you rat meat if they
could get away with it.
Just like the trumpet.

Milk

On the Milky Way's
breast of day
I sleep
and
awaken gazing into the stars
I open my eyes I see yours gazing back
tender as them stars up in heaven.
Forever cold
they do not fall
but closer
closer still
the twinkle is
consumed.
And I am lost in your warmth
again.

Escort

These lips of yours send me, darling.
They send me adrift on an ancient breeze
for which they have starved us all
and leave us without hunger
for a while.

Have it My Way

I see your sultry smile,
and smoky eyes
I fall for you.
I see your curves,
wanton and glistening,
inviting me to play on them.
My arms, starved to know how you will feel pressed against
me,
ache because they are empty
for now.
Your truth, so straight,
dares me to dance with your words,
fill you with sweet liquor
so that they will bend and swivel
like your hips held tight in the palms of my hands.
And when I ask you to dance
while it rains on a Sunday
I will trace every line of that sweet
sassy mouth with the very tip of my finger
I will taste your lips…relieve them of their suffering.
And then…
I will hold your head and play with your hair until you fall
asleep
and watch you dreaming up what we could have been.

Mr. Law

The very names tell me everything about thee.
L Is a long and lean letter, with feet like a clown's.
A You are so pointed.
W You confuse me with your double V's.
When I bring you together the word itself fizzles out, as if
it were an orange soda, left in sun to languish in its own
watered-down stew.
I say these things in word only.
To the man…a karate master, knowing that if I use bone and
flesh, he will contort my spine into a pretty red bow.
So I am a careful poet.
I use words.
Yes, yes, I know that he is a master of words as well.
But what master would knowingly accept a W at the end of
a surname?
Sir?!
I ask you to explain this to us?
I demand it!
And when you do, tell us with the eloquence of your second
master
not with a chop to the neck, or sword play, or an extended
fist through an eye socket.
Tell us using your second master.
The written word.

I dare you.

Mr. Hopson

(Mr. Law's response)

Hop. Son.
Imperative, a command,
a demand and call for action,
an arbitrary reaction to the fact of your existence.
I will speak and you will listen:
he says HOP, son
and you jump.
Hopson...
Son of Hop...
a short trip
to spring or leap.
A twining vine with tasty tendrils,
son of the winding sojourn, brother to the flutter of the
eastern breeze,
a tricksome traveler with adventure in his eyes.
Hopson,
The W in my name is for many things.
Wanderlust is one you know,
but wit is what I choose to show!
I surf the surging ebb and flow
with tongue in cheek and eyes aglow,
on tides of Whitman, Hughes, and Poe.
So hop on,
Hopson,
and answer this: Why, if you craft your words with care,
would you put a preposition there,
dangling off into the air
as if you do not grammar fear?
Answer that
if you dare,
Hopson.

My World on Fire

In cosmic shards
leaves change colors and shed,
falling into
empty space

and my world is ablaze.

Listening to my lies,
my soul ripped,
breathing, from my body.
Following a cone of warmth and light
that started today and descends into a single point,
the beginning and end of us all.

But one day
when our guarantee
of tomorrow
does not come,
when consciousness of our senses departs,
still the world will burn.

Hipster's Hell...

You live on its skin
you hipster motherfuckers
like a tick
you drink its blood
and play in its wet kisses.
When you are happy
you dance on its hairy ball sack
and make love to the other ticks that live there.
When you are sad
you eat its raw heart.
And when you are full
you hide,
to sleep,
safely dreaming,
in a shroud of nonsense
and rain
and lies made of sugar.

I Never Told you

That night...
that night...
when you were off talking to the devil,
I was holding his hand.

That night...
that night...
you were on a trip, a solo journey into madness and the
business end of a rope.
That night
I was having coffee with a pretty little fuck angel.
But first, I watched our child heal in the shadow of five
mighty trees, swaying in the breeze of a fierce Seattle storm.
They did not break.
Nor did he.

That night...
that night...
he looked up at me, and giggled just before they put him
under.
Like you.
And before they brought him back, a woman with whom
I'd shared smoked salmon said she refused to believe the
outside
was a place where people could not share the fruits of the
world.
She was wrong, of course.
That night…
when you were ill, you easily shared your suffering
with a poor, frightened old man
who told you that he'd lost a loved one to the same disease.

That night…
that night…
he looked at you half in fright, half in disgust.
And me, when you sang our song to her.

That night...
that night.
Tonight I am left with half of you
the good half, I think,
but only half.
I am holding hands with a friendly ghost.
You cannot ride a bus into the city alone, but the people who
take care of you are charmed,
bedazzled by your goodness.
Perhaps, that day in the park, you were only attempting to
strangle the addict's dream of killing you,
for us.
That night.
That night.

Kelly Flynn

Morning light
touches her body
and I watch
the slow miracle
of meeting her eyes
as she awakens:
salted eyes, smoky with love.
Mine are smoky too
for they traveled a thousand miles before hers opened
over her shoulders, down her little belly
and now her hips are moving.
The palm of my hand
absorbs heat from her skin;
my eyes watch her body warm to life,
bathed in this glorious light.

A Poem from the Universe

The seed left the dandelion,
cast into time and space
a tiny organism.
Above it
the galaxies roamed in their darkness,
each a massive
orgasmic
sea,
silent to the seed,
but heard by many others.

The Start of Something New

(Eixid)

You stand before eternity,
before a massive wave
sent to you from stars
lost before the day,
a billion of them
seething in hot plasma,
exploding in silence,
waiting for your smile.
Is it a beach where you are standing
or the end of the world?

There is an azure sky
lonely as you.
The clouds don't care.
Nor does the rusted chain in the sand,
keeping us safe from nothing at all.

Now your hand is in your hair,
holding it out of your eyes for my look.
A simple smile;
you tell me
"Go ahead, say it.
It may break my heart,
but it's more likely
to break your own."
A poet is good for that.
And when you play
you are so serious, darling.
Holding back your joy
for whom? From whom?
You are free now,

standing in front of this azure sky
with me,
standing before these exploding stars,
the ones you adore.

They are only waiting
for your ashes.
You can't conquer bones.
Give them, you say,
but don't give them your wishes.
Wishes do not belong to stars.

The Sad Sound of Laughter

The saddest sound
A thorny crown
Went flying though our holy ground.

A windy sound that smelled of musk
Is now the sound that must be hushed
It frayed the fabric of our trust:

And through this sound
Our hearts unwound
And rained our tears upon the ground.

Where twice you came
To make the sound
That shed new light to kick around.

You laughed with him
(I heard it, too)
And saw you there,
My world anew.

And this is where
We now can see
How deeply spiteful you can be.

The sweat, the stain, the wrinkled brow
Is now our song that has been drowned.

The laugh
The blow
(And now you know)
The love, the fire
Here, apropos.

I Think of the Octopus

In my neighborhood, you are a soft fish, and the moon pulls at your blood, quickening your pulse. Eyes watch you from above and below, waiting. To hide your flesh, you slip under a rock, a piece of kelp, a rotting animal's corpse, your small brain paranoid over eyes you cannot see. Murderers and liars, sex fiends and lunatics—my neighborhood is filled with them.

There is the octopus, crouching, sliding, hiding, murder on his mind; excited by your breath, he is hungry. In the dying light of day, the stinging cells of the anemones glow orange; armed with poison and patience, they wait. There is the starfish, slow but treacherous. With his tube feet he'll rip a hole in your skin large enough to insert his stomach, digesting you alive. A loving mate entices you with perfumes cast on the cold current, and you follow, you die, your flesh used for the incubation of eggs.

Me-Quaw-Muoks Beach is but a short walk from my home, and when I am thirsty for blood, I go there to watch the tide pools.
Like an Arnold Schwarzenegger movie gone live, there are no outtakes. In the "tranquil" world of a tide pool, violence is a way of life, a necessity for survival in a world empty of all emotion.
For beachcombing, the swollen tides of the equinox are best. When the sun and moon combine to pull the sea away from land, intertidal marine organisms are forced to live closer together. Crevasses, dips, and holes hold pools of life left behind by the tide. "The tide waits for no one," it is said.
At night, when troubled by some troubling thing, I walk to my beach. From the slope of its shores comes a barrage of waves, stumbling, rumbling over the cobblestones. They

talk: swoosh, swoosh, they say to me. In the dyed-velvet sky, Venus watches Orion, and the moon is jealous. Each star shines off the smooth water in reflection, shimmering slightly, blurred like a mirage. To watch like the voyeur, I bring with me a flashlight; the beam is a tiny sun.
I spy an anxious crab, brandishing a claw at my sun like a threatening boxer. At first chance, scurrying backwards, it slips under a rock. You're not so tough, I whisper. Here is an old beer bottle, chipped and scratched, its label long ago washed away. In it, perhaps, I will find a baby octopus. Secluded in a bottle's dimensions, the intelligent invertebrate finds safety in solitude. I peer inside but find only sand. In the distance I hear the lonely barking of a sea lion gone stag.

To watch a tide pool is to watch my world. The lying colors of the cuttlefish, the waiting anemone, the predatory moon snail and its victim the clam: together in a tide pool they form a dynamic balance. Like yin and yang, some are violent, some passive.
I walk home, a hole in my shoe, and pass an iron fence. Its spikes point up like the crab's oversized claws. The black metal battlements surround a small Victorian home, all of its windows dark except one. I think of the octopus.

I Do

Alice
I remember you.
I do.
You, the brave one.
Alice
like a mountain is quiet
watching us in our cloudy youth,
your toes in the grass
as two rosy cheeks
bless us with your joy.
Your eyes glint
just for me
as you erupt in laughter.
In a forest once
you sat in a cheap-ass camping chair
the way a salamander would sit
who watches as the world's tidbits fly by to eat.
You listened
welcoming our thoughts with the fey smile of an outlaw
greedy as a jeweler for them.
I watch you now,
distant
and in the past,
not knowing how precious these moments would be.
Dear Alice.
There are souls like you in the world who attract
starving bees without even a sweet sigh after they are fed.
It must have been lonely, too,
to suffer the talkers without sorrow
but to listen is golden
and to hear is to bare.
I remember that about you.
I do.

Crazy Normal

Crazy Normal
How I wish
You would greet me
With a kiss.
Your hair is brown
Your care is fair
Why don't you date me
If you dare?
You hardly scream
You screen your dreams
You should date me, so it seems.
The way you walk
The way you talk
Hits me like an electric shock.
You hardly ever
Have endeavors
That are too complicated
Or too clever.
NPR is in your car
You drive right by my favorite bar
Without a clue
And like a shrew
You've never been to Katmandu.
Yes, my dear, now it's clear
Those jeans don't fit you in the rear.
So, you should date me
If you dare
Then I can start on my repair.

A Story To The Girl In The Black Dress With Eyes The Color Of A Rainy Seattle Day

Chapter I.

I am in your elevator.
Waiting to reach your floor. There are thirteen. The numbers enthrall me as they light up one by one. The doors open. There you are, dressed as Dorothy from the Wizard of Oz.

Chapter II.

Through a crystal haze, I admire you. You are dreamy, careless. You take chances. I have studied phenomena like you. I know what your eyes are asking. Binary stars are birthed by a single magellanic cloud. It is their destiny to be in orbit.

Chapter III.

Like a priestess-monk explaining relativity to a sacred cow, you speak to me. Your voice drags, corporeally. You have faith in the animal. You have faith that it can understand. You whisper your words in gentle clues, and then you laugh. You are broken, aren't you, darling? I do not answer. We walk into the warm night and talk about the stars. Look up! you say. Tell me what you see.

Chapter IV.

I see the future.

Chapter V.

It is a hot summer night, and the tall blonde grass has gone to seed. The Milky Way is ablaze; points of light jewels strung upon the stupendous sky. It captures us in time, an image I now cherish. Together, we unveil a staggering vision: the apocalypse is near. We are watching it burn lazy-hot diamonds into the velvet night. The truth warms us. We tell our dreams to the stars, one by one, and count so many that we run out of dreams to hang on them. Your lips are ruby red. Your hair is jet black and pinned into two tight braids. You open a bottle of champagne. To the end…of all these worlds, I say. We drink. And you breathe into my ear, I love you. Get used to it.

Chapter VI.

I'm sorry.

Chapter VII.

The next day, you are in a different dress. The one that you first put on in a store where a woman warned you in Spanish, You had better buy this dress, señorita. It was made for you! You make enchiladas for me and play your favorite songs. We dance and play like otters in the dark. STILF, you call me. Science Teacher I'd Like To Fuck.

Chapter VIII.

I don't tell you.

Chapter IX.

We meet in a coffee shop. My fickle heart is stricken.

Chapter X.

You threaten to bake a blackberry pie, and without warning, you will one day smash it in my face.

Chapter XI.

The stars have returned, and they are closer than we dreamed. As it turns out, my apocalypse was only the beginning of a new cloud of ash from which to make more stars. The distance has closed. My heart has healed. I am waiting for that pie in the face, my dear. I am waiting to taste it. And when I do, I will have a bottle of champagne with me. I will uncork it and toast the new stars in our skies that have been born from the ash. You will wear that amazing black dress and, swaddled in black silk and lace, I will spray the ambrosia onto your tasty body.

Chapter XII.

I love you.

Pull Me into Darkness

(Ivone)

(To be read in Portuguese for best results.)

First we laugh, then we dance;
you tell me stories
of the dark, wet jungle
from which you came,
the sounds of the animals
and the perfumed lust of plants I detect on your sugared
skin.
I will pour wine into your mouth
And steal it back into my own with kisses.
My hands on your hips,
I pull you closer
into darkness
into my bed.
I lay you on my finest sheets,
smell your neck,
touch you with the back of my hand,
starving my finger tips
of your silken skin.
I will save this pleasure for your breast
where the palm of my hands will be waiting.
My lips
will kiss the wine again
and write kisses that will become stanzas.
Hungry for the words
to eat
as you moan
I taste honey
which doth drip from the hive.

Leve-me a escuridão[1]

(Ivone)

Primeiro nós rimos
é depois dançamos,
e você me conta histórias sobre a floresta húmida da onde você veio.
O som dos animais,
e o perfumem das plantas luxuriantes,
o qual, eu sinto em sua doce pele.
Eu derramo vinho em sua boca,
Eu o bebo de volta
Lhe dando gentil beijos roubados.
Minha mãos em suas cadeiras, puxam você mais perto.

---

1   **Take Me to Darkness**

(Ivone)

First we laugh
Then we dance,
and you tell me stories about the rainforest from where you came.
The animal sounds,
and the perfumes of lush plants,
which, I feel on her sweet skin.
I pour wine into his mouth.
I drink it from it,
giving you gentle stolen kisses.
My hands pull you closer.
I take it in the darkness, the way you like it. I am lying in my bed, in my
best sheets.

Smell her neck.
The play with the back of my hand is killing the irresistible desire of my
fingers to touch your silky skin.
I will have that pleasure with her breasts. The palm of my hand waiting,
and my lips are in synthesis to kiss this wine again. To write the kisses
that will turn into pleasure traits.
Encouraged by the words, they eat their moans in my mouth tasting the
honey-dripping beehive.

Eu lhe levo a escuridão, do jeito que você gosta. Em minha cama deitada, em meus melhores lençóis .

Cheiro seu pescoço.
O toco com o dorso da minha mão, matando a vontade irresistível dos meus dedos de tocar sua pele de seda.
Eu terei esse prazer com seus peitos. A palma da minha mão aguarda, e meus lábios síntese com sede para beijar esse vinho outra vez. Para escrever os beijos que vão se transformar em traços de prazer,
Fomentos pelas palavras, eles comem seu gemidos em minha boca: provando o mel que pinga da colmeia.

Signal Mountain

The great escape
in broad daylight
into thine own self
infinitely tangled...
straight into the face of god.

Alone
to see
to judge
the disasters
of life.

A conversation
with feral poets
who see as far as the night

and further still

where their ideas are
shouted

into the cannon
into destiny
into fire
into wounds
that heal into scars
and are opened again.

Thus is the beginning
found on a mountain
with light
streaming from some
unseen place.

And there you are
A signal,
A revelation.

Only Me, Fair May

I think you know it.
The teasing is my clue.
You peeking in on me
like a cat in sunshine,
mouse in paw.

There is no harm in telling you this:
you are ethereal
and the medium you breathe
is the tiniest of miracles
wandering through your curious mind.

Sometimes, with your chin in your hand,
you think about these things,
the wanton, wishful men who dream of you.
Yet they are left only with your puzzle.
And that is fine.
It is part of what makes you irresistible.

But time is an evil bastard.
He is restless.
He doesn't shave
or play the game.
And he doesn't tell lies to pretty girls.
Only truth.
Like you,
he rests his chin in his hand,
lighting matches and watching them burn.

Redwing

You charmed us
in the way you do
into an old Victorian on Redwing.
"Who are you going to believe?
A gut instinct?
Or a singer-song writer with magical eyes?"
Like me, that sweet, darling, old woman whose husband had
just passed
never stood a chance.
It was she versus you.
She suspected we'd mess up the place.
And we did.
First thing: tear down the velvet wallpaper, purple with
delicate flowers pressed into it.
Next thing: replace the shaggy carpet,
orange like Alabama clay,
sending up clouds of dust when we walked on it.
It had to go before the boy came.
His heart couldn't take it.
You were nesting,
A force of nature.
We had a library there and five rooms to make love in.
In the summer we'd choose the coolest floor to haunt.
When the nest of ladybugs hatched in our steamy bath, we
knew we'd meet our son soon. We never used the nursery
we made.
The boy slept with us, a little pterodactyl
right under our wings.
There are too many memories to thaw
a frozen mist carried in time and encased and blown though
fields of stars.
My mind can do amazing things with the patterns:
turn the grains into constellations in the sky.

Devils and angels.
Objects.
I study them now and withdraw further from our riches.
The house, our second child, the dusty furniture we never
rested on.
Pictures of your family on the mantle: slave owners
Sitting next to mine: slaves,
and now our little ones sweeten our ancestors' blood.
Bees drinking nectar.
And these are they, the dreams and mysteries, the wishes
and abominations of that time in our home, the nest that was
as it seems to me
down the quiet street,
Covered by trees.
Under the wisteria.
Dwelling on serum
and dewed autumn grass
'neath the balustrade
thither
and through the indigo door with a sticky lock.

Peach on a Tree

(A Note to Eve)

Not an apple...
a peach.
By design, better than an apple.
It is to be seized, savored
and rollicked on the tongue,
its nectar rived and quaffed.
Not the apple,
bitten and chewed
the way a cow masticates cud.
No. A peach is relished.
Silk on the skin, a sweet, slow game of
ambuscade!
Eve was wrong to choose the apple.
Perhaps the peach tree was hidden in another part
Of God's garden,
A place where she could not find it,
behind a wall of figs or mangos.
She'd never look there.
Had she done so, the bite would have been worth it.
She'd have kept her tears at bay.
Adam would have understood,
And so would his father.
We'd be thanking her instead.

What May Come, Will Come

Lie down here
and carelessly wait
for the sound
of marching happiness.

In a field
of wayward waiting,
soaked in sugar,
laughter,
and musk,

lie down here
and rest
with these
seraphic, blooming weeds.

Wait…
with me,
as cherubs do
and listen to the sound
of thunder rolling in.

OTHER ANAPHORA LITERARY PRESS TITLES

Film Theory and Modern Art
Editor: Anna Faktorovich

Interview with Larry Niven
Editor: Anna Faktorovich

Dragonflies in the Cowburbs
Donelle Dreese

Domestic Subversive
Roberta Salper

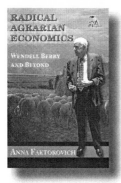

Radical Agrarian Economics
Anna Faktorovich

Fajitas and Beer Convention
Roger Rodriguez

Spirit of Tabasco
Richard Diedrichs

Skating in Concord
Jean LeBlanc

CPSIA information can be obtained at www.ICGtesting.com
Printed in the USA
LVOW12s1301150615

442425LV00061BA/542/P